Impacts of Visitor Spending on the Local Economy

Congaree National Park, 2011

Natural Resource Report NPS/NRSS/EQD/NRR—2013/613

Philip S. Cook

Visitor Services Project
Park Studies Unit
University of Idaho
Moscow, ID 83844-1139

January 2013

U.S. Department of the Interior
National Park Service
Natural Resource Stewardship and Science
Fort Collins, Colorado

The National Park Service, Natural Resource Stewardship and Science office in Fort Collins, Colorado, publishes a range of reports that address natural resource topics. These reports are of interest and applicability to a broad audience in the National Park Service and others in natural resource management, including scientists, conservation and environmental constituencies, and the public.

The Natural Resource Report Series is used to disseminate high-priority, current natural resource management information with managerial application. The series targets a general, diverse audience, and may contain NPS policy considerations or address sensitive issues of management applicability.

All manuscripts in the series receive the appropriate level of peer review to ensure that the information is scientifically credible, technically accurate, appropriately written for the intended audience, and designed and published in a professional manner.

Data in this report were collected and analyzed using methods based on established, peer-reviewed protocols and were analyzed and interpreted within the guidelines of the protocols.

Views, statements, findings, conclusions, recommendations, and data in this report do not necessarily reflect views and policies of the National Park Service, U.S. Department of the Interior. Mention of trade names or commercial products does not constitute endorsement or recommendation for use by the U.S. Government.

This report is available from the Social Science Division (http://www.nature.nps.gov/socialscience/index.cfm) and the Natural Resource Publications Management website (http://www.nature.nps.gov/publications/nrpm/).

This report and other reports by the Visitor Services Project (VSP) are available from the VSP website (http://www.psu.uidaho.edu/c5/vsp/vsp-reports/) or by contacting the VSP office at (208) 885-7863.

Please cite this publication as:

Cook, P. S. 2013. Impacts of visitor spending on the local economy: Congaree National Park, 2011. Natural Resource Report NPS/NRSS/EQD/NRR—2013/613. National Park Service, Fort Collins, Colorado.

NPS 178/119428, January 2013

Contents

Figures

Tables

Appendices

Executive Summary

Congaree National Park hosted 120,166 recreation visits in 2011. Adjustments for visitor group size and re-entries resulted in 46,743 visitor group trips to the park in 2011. Based on four Visitor Services Project surveys conducted May 2–15, 2011, July 27 – August 19, 2011, October 27 – November 27, 2011, and January 27 – March 7, 2012, 60% of visitor group trips were made by local residents or non-locals on day trips, not including an overnight stay within a one-hour drive of the park.[1]

Visitors reported their group's expenditures inside the park and within a one-hour drive of the park. The average visitor group was 2.5 people in size and spent an average of $4.66 inside the park and an average of $114.10 outside the park within a one-hour drive.

Total visitor spending in 2011 in the park and within a one-hour drive of the park was $5.6 million, including $218,000 inside the park. The greatest proportion of expenditures was for overnight accommodations (32%). Overnight visitors staying in lodges, hotels, motels, cabins, B&Bs, etc. in the local area accounted for 68% of total spending.

Sixty-four percent of visitor groups indicated the park visit was the primary reason for their trip to the area. Counting only a portion of visitor expenses if the park visit was not the primary reason for the trip yields $4.4 million in spending attributed directly to the park.

The economic impact of park visitor spending was estimated by applying the spending to an input-output model of the local economy. The local region was defined as a six-county region including Richland, Calhoun, Orangeburg, Clarendon, Sumter, and Lexington counties, South Carolina. This region roughly coincides with the one-hour driving radius around the park for which expenditures were reported.

Including direct and secondary effects, the $4.4 million in visitor spending attributed to the park generated $5.6 million in direct sales in the region, which supported 75 jobs. These jobs paid $1.9 million in labor income, which was part of $3.1 million in value added to the region.[2]

A separate study estimated impacts of the park employee payroll on the local economy.[3] The park itself employed 24 people in FY 2010 with a total payroll including benefits of $1.4 million. Including secondary effects, the local impacts of the park payroll in FY 2010 were $750,000 in sales, supporting 31 jobs, $1.6 million in labor income, and $1.8 million in value added.

Local Economic Impacts of Congaree National Park				
	Sales	Jobs	Labor Income	Value Added
Park Visitor Spending	$5.6M	75	$1.9M	$3.1M
Park Payroll	+ $0.7M	+ 31	+ $1.6M	+ $1.8M
Park Visitor Spending + Payroll	$6.3M	106	$3.5M	$4.9M

---

[1] Results in this study sometimes differ from those reported in the VSP study reports (Kulesza 2012a, 2012b; Samuelson 2012a, 2012b) for two reasons. First, the results in this report adjust for seasonal differences in visitor group trip characteristics and combine data from the four VSP surveys. Second, the current analysis excludes some cases as outliers. See Study Limitations and Errors section and Appendix D.

[2] Jobs include fulltime and part-time jobs. Labor income consists of wages and salaries, payroll benefits and income of sole proprietors. Value added includes labor income as well as property income (dividend, royalties, interest and rents) to area businesses and indirect business taxes (sales, property, and excise taxes).

[3] Stynes (2011).

Acknowledgments

The author thanks Margaret Littlejohn, Visitor Services Project Director, for her review of an early draft of this report.

Introduction

Congaree National Park (NP) preserves the largest intact expanse of old growth hardwood forest remaining in the southeastern United States. The 26,000-acre park is located in Richland County, South Carolina. Congaree NP received 120,166 recreation visits in 2011, including 5,503 overnight stays (Table 1).

Table 1. Recreation visits and overnight stays, Congaree National Park, 2011

Month	Recreation visits	Overnight (OVN) Stays		
		Backcountry campers	Group campers	Total OVN stays
January	6,657	30	191	221
February	8,621	190	596	786
March	12,582	159	718	877
April	11,277	102	617	719
May	11,215	43	318	361
June	11,689	92	154	246
July	3,233	72	141	213
August	11,117	10	144	154
September	15,493	47	366	413
October	11,676	133	482	615
November	9,825	184	301	485
December	6,781	114	299	413
Total	**120,166**	**1,176**	**4,327**	**5,503**

Source: NPS Public Use Statistics 2011.

The purpose of this study is to estimate the annual, local economic impacts of visitors to Congaree NP in 2011. Economic impacts are measured as the direct and secondary sales, income, and jobs in the local region resulting from spending by park visitors. (See Appendix A: Glossary for definitions of terms.) In addition, a separate study estimated the impacts of the NPS park payroll on the local region (Stynes 2011), and those results are reported herein. Neither study estimated the economic impacts of park operations or construction spending on the local region.

The local economic region defined for this study includes Richland, Calhoun, Orangeburg, Clarendon, Sumter, and Lexington counties, South Carolina. This six-county region has a population of 896,998 (USCB 2010), gross regional product of $34.9 billion (MIG, Inc. 2008), median household income of $49,365, and family poverty rate of 11.7% (USCB 2010). State and local governments, including education, and food services and drinking places are the major employers in the region (MIG, Inc. 2008), and the region experienced a 9.7% unemployment rate in 2011 (BLS 2010).

Methods

The economic impact estimates are produced using the Money Generation Model 2 (MGM2) (Stynes et al. 2007). The three main inputs to the model are:

1. number of visits broken down by lodging-based segments;
2. spending averages for each segment; and
3. economic multipliers for the local region.

Inputs are estimated from Congaree NP Visitor Services Project (VSP) survey data (Kulesza et al. 2012a, 2012b, Samuelson et al. 2012a, 2012b), National Park Service Public Use Statistics (2011), and IMPLAN input-output modeling software (MIG, Inc. 2008). The MGM2 model provides a spreadsheet template for combining park use, spending, and regional multipliers to compute changes in sales, labor income, jobs, and value added in the region.

The VSP visitor surveys were conducted at Congaree NP from May 2–15, 2011 (spring), July 27 – August 19, 2011 (summer), October 27 – November 27, 2011 (fall), and January 27 – March 7, 2012 (winter).[4] The VSP surveys measured visitor demographics, activities, and travel expenditures. Questionnaires were distributed to a systematic, random sample of 450 visitor groups in spring 2011, 448 visitor groups in summer 2011, 452 visitor groups in fall 2011, and 446 visitor groups in winter 2012. Response rates were 69.6%, 61.2%, 72.8%, and 76.5%, respectively.

Spending and economic impact estimates for Congaree NP are based on the spring 2011, summer 2011, fall 2011, and winter 2012 VSP survey data. Spending averages for spring visitor groups were estimated using the spring 2011 VSP survey data and applied to visitor groups between March and May. Spending averages for summer visitor groups were estimated using the summer 2011 VSP survey data and applied to visitor groups between June and August. Spending averages for fall visitor groups were estimated using the fall 2011 VSP survey data and applied to visitor groups between September and November. Winter visitor group spending averages were estimated using the winter 2012 VSP survey data and assumed to represent visitor groups from December through February. Although winter visitor spending data were collected in January – March 2012, spending averages and patterns are assumed to apply to all winter visitors in 2011.

Visitors were asked to report expenditures within a one-hour drive of the park. The local region for determining economic impact was defined as a six-county area around the park including Richland, Calhoun, Orangeburg, Clarendon, Sumter, and Lexington counties, South Carolina, which roughly coincides with the one-hour driving radius for which visitor spending was reported.

---

[4] Results in this study sometimes differ from those reported in the VSP study reports (Kulesza at al. 2012a, 2012b, Smauelson et al. 2012a, 2012b) because of the omission of cases considered to be outliers in the current analysis. See Study Limitations and Errors section.

The MGM2 model divides visitors into segments to help explain differences in spending across distinct user groups. Six segments were established for Congaree NP visitors based on reported trip characteristics and lodging expenditures:

Local: Visitors from the local region, not staying overnight inside the park.

Day trip: Visitors from outside the local region, not staying overnight within a one-hour drive of the park.

Camp-in: Visitors reporting camping inside the park.

Motel-out: Visitors reporting motel expenses within a one-hour drive of the park.[5]

Camp-out: Visitors reporting camping expenses outside the park within a one-hour drive of the park.

Other overnight (Other OVN): Visitors staying overnight in the local region but not reporting any lodging expenses. This segment includes visitors staying in private homes, with friends or relatives, or in other unpaid lodging.[6]

The VSP survey data were used to estimate the percentage of visitors from each segment as well as spending averages, lengths of stay, and visitor group sizes for each segment. Segment shares from the VSP surveys were adjusted to be consistent with the park's NPS Public Use Statistics (2011) overnight stay figures.

---

[5] The questionnaire asked about expenditures for "Lodges, hotels, motels, cabins, B&B, etc." For convenience, these expenditures are referred to as "motel" in this report.

[6] Visitors reporting multiple lodging types and expenditures were classified based on the greatest reported lodging expense. Some visitors listing motels or campgrounds as lodging types did not report any lodging expenses and were classified in the other overnight (Other OVN) category.

Results

Visits

Based on the VSP survey data, 62% of park entries were classified as day trip visits by either local residents or visitors from outside the local region, and the remaining 38% were classified as overnight visits including an overnight stay in the local region (Table 2). The average visitor group size ranged from 2.3 to 2.8 people across the six segments with an average visitor group of 2.5 people.[7] The average length of stay in the local region on overnight trips was 1.9 nights.

Table 2. Selected visit/trip characteristics by segment, 2011

	Segment						
Characteristic	Local	Day trip	Camp-in	Motel-out	Camp-out	Other OVN	All visitors
Visitor segment share (park entries)	30%	32%	5%	21%	2%	9%	100%
Average visitor group size	2.6	2.6	2.8	2.3	2.4	2.4	2.5
Length of stay (days or nights)	1.0	1.0	1.1	1.8	1.9	2.3	1.9
Re-entry rate (park entries per trip)	1.0	1.0	1.2	1.0	1.1	1.2	1.0
Percent primary purpose trips	100%	70%	93%	62%	64%	47%	64%

Sixty-four percent of visitor groups indicated that visiting the park was the primary reason for their trip to the area. Other stated reasons included visiting friends and relatives in the area, business, traveling through, or visiting other area attractions.

The 120,166 recreation visits in 2011 were allocated to the six segments using the visit segment shares in Table 2. Because spending is reported for the stay in the area, recreation visits were converted to visitor group trips to the area by dividing recreation visits by the average number of times each visitor entered the park during their stay and the average visitor group size. Park re-entry rates were estimated based on the number of days survey respondents reported visiting the park, assuming one entry per day. The 120,166 recreation visits represented 46,743 visitor group trips (Table 3).

Table 3. Recreation visits and visitor group trips by segment, 2011

	Segment						
Measure	Local	Day trip	Camp-in	Motel-out	Camp-out	Other OVN	All visitors
Recreation visits	35,986	38,515	5,798	25,587	2,923	11,356	120,166
Visitor group trips	13,762	14,620	1,974	10,964	1,289	4,135	46,743
Percent of visitor group trips*	29%	31%	4%	23%	3%	9%	100%

*Segment percentages do not total 100% due to rounding.

---

[7] Visitor group size reported herein is based on the number of people covered by expenditures reported in the VSP surveys.

Visitor Spending

The VSP survey collected data about expenditures of visitor groups inside the park and within a one-hour drive of the park.[8] Spending averages were computed on a visitor group trip basis for each segment. Spending averages for the year were computed by weighting seasonal spending averages by the percentage of visits occurring during each season (spring, summer, fall, or winter; see Appendix D).

The average visitor group spent $119 on the trip inside the park and in the local region (Table 4). On a visitor group trip basis, average spending was $23 for day trips by local residents and $48 for day trips by non-local visitors. Visitor groups staying in motels spent an average of $342 on their trips. Visitor groups camping in the park spent an average of $65 on their trips, while visitor groups camping outside the park spent an average of $249 on their trips. Visitor groups spent about 4% of their total spending inside the park and 96% outside the park.

Table 4. Average spending by segment , 2011 (dollars per visitor group per trip)

Expenditures	Segment						
	Local	Day trip	Camp-in	Motel-out	Camp-out	Other OVN	All visitors*
Inside park							
Souvenirs & other expenses	2.75	4.45	4.55	6.47	6.66	6.39	4.66
Total inside park	**2.75**	**4.45**	**4.55**	**6.47**	**6.66**	**6.39**	**4.66**
Outside park							
Motels	0.00	0.00	0.00	156.56	0.00	0.00	36.72
Camping fees	0.00	0.00	0.00	0.07	49.96	0.00	1.39
Restaurants & bars	5.04	11.48	11.13	72.98	26.37	16.76	24.87
Groceries & takeout food	3.55	3.64	11.42	11.74	35.43	14.42	7.67
Gas & oil	8.99	22.36	24.92	54.54	90.50	30.45	28.67
Local transportation	0.06	1.62	0.00	18.31	11.47	0.89	5.21
Admission & fees	1.25	2.19	0.29	6.98	16.42	2.55	3.38
Souvenirs & other expenses	1.44	2.46	13.10	14.58	12.21	7.56	6.17
Total outside park	**20.34**	**43.74**	**60.85**	**335.76**	**242.37**	**72.63**	**114.10**
Total inside & outside park	**23.09**	**48.19**	**65.40**	**342.23**	**249.03**	**79.02**	**118.76**

*Weighted by percent visitor group trips.

The relative standard error at a 95% confidence level for the overall spending average is 11%. A 95% confidence interval for the overall visitor group spending average is therefore $119 plus or minus $13 or between $106 and $132.

---

[8] Some expenditure categories in the VSP questionnaire were combined for reporting herein and MGM2 analysis. See Appendix B.

On a per night basis, visitor groups staying in motels spent $195 in the local region, and campers outside the park spent $129 (Table 5). The average reported per-night lodging expense was $89 for motels and $26 for camping fees outside the park.

Table 5. Average spending per night for visitor groups on overnight trips, 2011 (dollars per visitor group per night)

Expenditures	Segment			
	Camp-in	Motel-out	Camp-out	Other OVN
Motels	0.00	89.00	0.00	0.00
Camping fees	0.00	0.04	25.92	0.00
Restaurants & bars	10.58	41.49	13.68	7.43
Groceries & takeout food	10.86	6.68	18.39	6.39
Gas & oil	23.71	31.00	46.96	13.50
Local transportation	0.00	10.41	5.95	0.40
Admission & fees	0.28	3.97	8.52	1.13
Souvenirs & other expenses	16.78	11.97	9.79	6.19
Total per visitor group per night	**62.21**	**194.55**	**129.23**	**35.03**

Total spending was estimated by multiplying the number of visitor group trips for each segment by the average spending per trip and summing across segments. Congaree NP visitors spent a total of $5.6 million in the local region in 2011 (Table 6). Overnight visitors staying in motels accounted for 68% of the total spending. Motel expenses represented 31% of the total spending (Figure 1).

Table 6. Total visitor spending by segment, 2011 (thousands of dollars)

Expenditures	Segment						All visitors
	Local	Day trip	Camp-in	Motel-out	Camp-out	Other OVN	
Inside park							
Souvenirs & other expenses	38	65	9	71	9	26	218
Total inside park	**38**	**65**	**9**	**71**	**9**	**26**	**218**
Outside park							
Motels	0	0	0	1,717	0	0	1,717
Camping fees	0	0	0	1	64	0	65
Restaurants & bars	69	168	22	800	34	69	1,163
Groceries & takeout food	49	53	23	129	46	60	359
Gas & oil	124	327	49	598	117	126	1,340
Local transportation	1	24	0	201	15	4	244
Admission & fees	17	32	1	77	21	11	158
Souvenirs & other expenses	20	36	26	160	16	31	288
Total outside park	**280**	**639**	**120**	**3,681**	**312**	**300**	**5,333**
Total inside & outside park	**318**	**705**	**129**	**3,752**	**321**	**327**	**5,551**
Segment percent of total*	6%	13%	2%	68%	6%	6%	100%

*Segment percentages do not total 100% due to rounding.

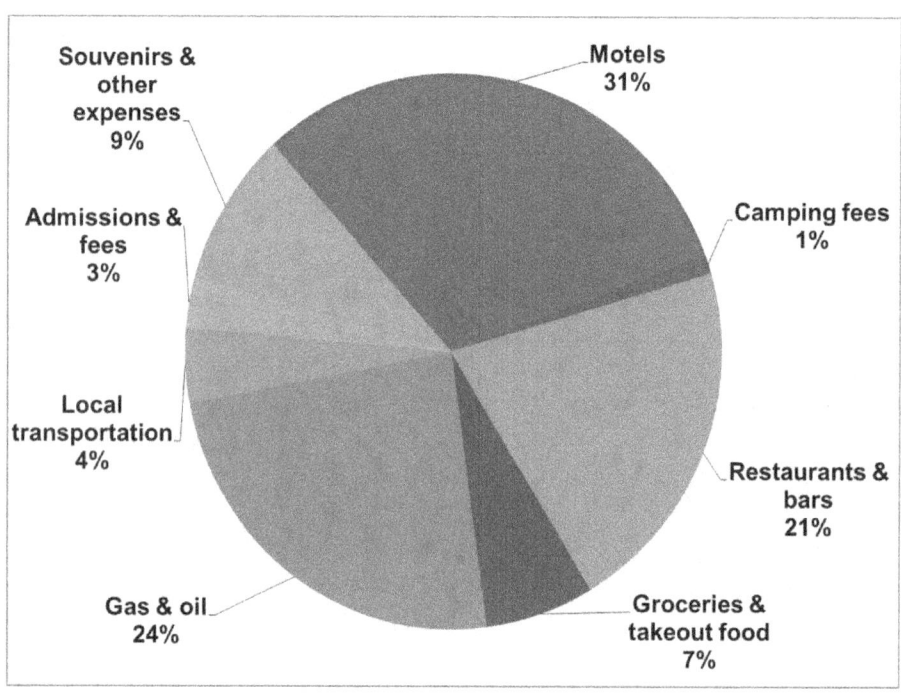

Figure 1. Congaree NP visitor spending by category, 2011

Because visitors would come to the region whether or not the park existed, not all visitor spending can be attributed to the park. Thirty-six percent of visitor groups did not make the trip primarily to visit Congaree NP. Spending directly attributed to park visits was estimated by counting all spending on trips for which the park was the primary reason for the trip. If the park was not the primary trip purpose, one night of spending was counted for overnight trips and half of the spending in the region was counted for day trips. All spending inside the park was treated as park-related spending. With these assumptions, a total of $4.4 million in visitor spending was attributed to park visits (Table 7). This represented 80% of the overall visitor spending total.

Table 7. Total spending attributed to park visits, 2011 (thousands of dollars)

	Segment						
Expenditures	Local	Day trip	Camp-in	Motel-out	Camp-out	Other OVN	All visitors
Motels	0	0	0	1,437	0	0	1,437
Camping fees	0	0	0	1	53	0	54
Restaurants & bars	0	142	22	670	28	49	911
Groceries & takeout food	0	45	22	108	38	42	255
Gas & oil	0	277	49	500	97	88	1012
Local transportation	0	20	0	168	12	3	203
Admission & fees	0	27	1	64	18	7	117
Souvenirs & other expenses	38	96	35	205	22	48	443
Total attributed to park	**38**	**607**	**129**	**3,152**	**268**	**237**	**4,431**
Percent of spending attributed to the park	12%	86%	100%	84%	83%	73%	80%
Percent of attributed spending	1%	14%	3%	71%	6%	5%	100%

Economic Impacts of Visitor Spending

The economic impacts of Congaree NP visitor spending on the local economy were estimated by applying visitor spending to a set of economic ratios and multipliers in MGM2 representing the economy of the six-county region—Richland, Calhoun, Orangeburg, Clarendon, Sumter, and Lexington counties, South Carolina.[9] Economic ratios and multipliers for the region were estimated using the *Impact Analysis for Planning (IMPLAN) Professional software* (version 3, MIG, Inc. 2008) with 2008 data.[10] Multipliers were updated to take into account price changes from 2008 to 2011 (see Study Limitations and Errors section below).

Not all visitor spending was counted as direct sales to the region. The amount a visitor spends for a retail good is made up of the cost of the good from the producer, a markup by a wholesaler, and a markup by a retailer. In MGM2, retail and wholesale margins for grocery & takeout food, gas & oil, and souvenirs & other expenses are applied to visitor spending to account for mark-ups by retailers and wholesalers. The retail margins for the three sectors are 25.3%, 22.3%, and 50.0%, respectively, and the wholesale margins are 12.3%, 8.3%, and 11.4%. In addition, regional purchase coefficients from IMPLAN for all sectors are used to account for the proportion of demand within the region satisfied by imports into the region.

The tourism output sales multiplier for the region was 1.63. Every dollar of direct sales to visitors generated another $0.63 in secondary sales through indirect and induced effects.[11] (See Appendix A: Glossary for further explanation of terms.)

The economic impacts to the local region are presented in two ways: (1) based on all visitor spending and (2) based only on visitor spending attributable to the park. The first estimate—including all visitor spending—shows the overall contribution park visitors make to the local region. The second estimate—including only visitor spending attributable to the park—shows the impact or contribution the park makes to the economy of the local region.

---

[9] Economic ratios convert between various economic measures, e.g., direct spending to the directly associated jobs, labor income, and value added in each sector. Economic multipliers capture the secondary effects of economic measures.

[10] See Appendix C: Economic Ratios and Multipliers for the region.

[11] Indirect effects result from tourism businesses buying goods and services from local firms, while induced effects stem from household spending of income earned from visitor spending.

Impacts of All Visitor Spending

Using all visitor spending and including direct and secondary effects, the $5.6 million spent by park visitors generated $6.9 million in sales, which supported 93 jobs in the local region (Table 8). These jobs paid $2.3 million in labor income, which was part of $3.9 million in value added to the region.[12]

Table 8. Impacts of all visitor spending on the local economy, 2011*

Sector/expenditure category	Sales (thousands of dollars)	Jobs	Labor income (thousands of dollars)	Value added (thousands of dollars)
Direct effects				
Motels	1,717	23.3	514	916
Camping fees	65	0.8	21	34
Restaurants & bars	1,163	22.3	399	568
Groceries & takeout food	91	1.7	47	76
Gas & oil	299	5.4	150	249
Local transportation	244	7.6	105	132
Admission & fees	158	3.0	59	90
Souvenirs & other expenses	253	5.3	129	211
Wholesale trade	203	1.2	77	133
Local production of goods	46	0.1	3	6
Total direct effects	**4,238**	**70.6**	**1,504**	**2,414**
Secondary effects	2,687	22.4	823	1,450
Total effects	**6,925**	**93.0**	**2,327**	**3,864**

*Note: Impacts of $5.6 million in visitor spending reported in Table 6. Totals may not equal sum of individual categories due to rounding.

Value added is the preferred measure of the contribution of visitors to the local economy as it includes all sources of income to the area—payroll benefits to workers, profits and rents to businesses, and sales and other indirect business taxes that accrue to government units. Value added impacts are also comparable to Gross Regional Product, the broadest measure of total economic activity in a region. The largest direct effects are in restaurants & bars and motels.

Impacts of Visitor Spending Attributed to the Park

Using only visitor spending attributable to the park by including only some spending on trips where the primary trip purpose was not to visit Congaree NP reduces the overall impacts by about 19% (Table 9; see spending inclusion assumptions in previous section). Including direct and secondary effects, the $4.4 million spent by park visitors and attributable to the park generated $5.6 million in sales, which supported 75 jobs in the local region. These jobs paid $1.9 million in labor income, which was part of $3.1 million in value added to the region.

---

[12] Jobs include full and part time jobs. Labor income consists of wages and salaries, payroll benefits and income of sole proprietors. Value added includes labor income as well as profits and rents to area businesses and sales and excise taxes.

Table 9. Economic impacts of visitor spending attributed to the park, 2011*

Sector/expenditure category	Sales (thousands of dollars)	Jobs	Labor income (thousands of dollars)	Value added (thousands of dollars)
Direct effects				
Motels	1,437	19.5	431	766
Camping fees	54	0.6	17	28
Restaurants & bars	911	17.5	312	445
Groceries & takeout food	65	1.2	33	54
Gas & oil	226	4.1	113	188
Local transportation	203	6.3	87	110
Admission & fees	117	2.2	43	66
Souvenirs & other expenses	221	4.6	113	184
Wholesale trade	158	0.9	60	103
Local production of goods	36	0.1	3	5
Total direct effects	**3,427**	**57.0**	**1,213**	**1,950**
Secondary effects	2,175	18.2	666	1,174
Total effects	**5,602**	**75.2**	**1,880**	**3,124**

*Note: Impacts of $4.4 million in visitor spending attributed to park reported in Table 7. Totals may not equal sum of individual categories due to rounding.

Economic Impacts of the NPS Park Payroll

In addition to visitor spending, spending by park employees also impacts the local region. A separate study (Stynes 2011) estimated the impacts of park payroll by applying economic multipliers to wage and salary data to capture the induced effects of NPS employee spending on local economies. Congaree NP itself employed 24 people in FY 2010 with a total payroll including benefits of $1.4 million.[13] Including secondary effects, the local impacts of the park payroll in FY 2010 were $750,000 in sales, 31 jobs, $1.6 million in labor income, and $1.8 million value added (Stynes 2011).

Combined Economic Impacts

The combined impacts to the region of visitor spending attributable to the park and NPS payroll were $6.3 million in sales, which supported 106 jobs with labor income of $3.5 million, which was part of a total value added of $4.9 million.

---

[13] The number of employees was estimated by totaling the number of distinct social security numbers in each pay period and dividing by the number of pay periods. The figure is therefore an annual average. Four seasonal jobs for three months count as one job. No distinction is made between part-time and full-time employees. Jobs, salary, and payroll benefits are assigned to the park where the employee's time was charged, which may differ from their duty station (Stynes 2011).

Study Limitations and Errors

The accuracy of the MGM2 estimates rests on the accuracy of three inputs: visits, spending averages, and multipliers. Visits are taken from NPS Public Use Statistics (2010). Recreation visit estimates rely on counting procedures at the park, which may miss some visitors and count others more than once during their visit. Re-entry rates are important to adjust the park visit counts to reflect the number of visitor group trips to the region rather than park entries. Re-entry rates were estimated based on the number of days the respondent reported visiting the park and assuming one park entry per day.

Spending averages are derived from the spring 2011, summer 2011, fall 2011, and winter 2012 Congaree NP VSP visitor surveys (Kolesza et al. 2012a, 2012b; Samuelson et al. 2012a, 2012b). Estimates from the surveys are subject to sampling and measurement errors. The overall spending average is subject to a sampling error of 11%.

Spending averages are also sensitive to decisions about outliers and treatment of missing data. In order to estimate spending averages, incomplete spending data were filled with zeros. Visitor groups of more than 8 people (4 cases in summer sample, 3 cases in summer sample, 12 cases in fall sample, 6 cases in winter sample) or visiting the local region for more than 7 nights (4 cases in spring sample, 7 cases in summer sample, 3 cases in fall sample, 2 cases in winter sample) were omitted from the analysis. In addition visitor groups with total spending more than $1,068 in the spring sample (11 cases), $1,215 in the summer sample (9 cases), $867 in the fall sample (10 cases), and $655 in the winter sample (13 cases; the mean for each sample plus two times the standard deviation of the mean for spending) were omitted from the analysis. These are conservative assumptions about outliers and likely result in conservative estimates of economic impacts.

Visitors sampled during each sampling period were assumed to represent visitors throughout their respective seasons. To extrapolate to annual totals, it was assumed that the spring sample represented visitors from March thru May, the summer sample represented visitors from June thru August, the fall sample represented visitors from September thru November, and the winter sample represented visitors from December thru February. Visitors in the winter sample (January 27 – March 7, 2012) were assumed to be similar to winter visitors throughout 2011.

Multipliers are derived from an input-output model of the local economy using IMPLAN (MIG, Inc. 2008). The basic assumptions of input-output models are that sectors have homogeneous, fixed and linear production functions, that prices are constant, and that there are no supply constraints. The IMPLAN system uses national average production functions for each of 440 sectors based on the NAICS system (see Appendix B, Table B2). The most recent local IMPLAN datasets available for this analysis were 2008. National IMPLAN multiplier data were available for 2009, so local employment, labor income, and value added multipliers were updated to 2009 using 2008/2009 national ratios. In addition, local employment multipliers were updated to 2011 based on changes in consumer price indices.

Sorting out how much spending to attribute to the park when the park is not the primary reason for the trip is somewhat subjective. Because 36% of visitor groups to Congaree NP did not make the trip primarily to visit the park and most spending occurred outside the park, adjustments for non-primary purpose trips have a significant effect on the overall spending and impact estimates.

Literature Cited

BLS (U.S. Bureau of Labor Statistics). 2011. Local Area Unemployment Statistics. http://www.bls.gov/lau/. Data retrieved on September 26, 2012.

Kulesza, C., Y. Le, and S.J. Hollenhorst. 2012a. Congaree National Park Visitor Study, Spring 2011. Natural Resource Report NPS/NRSS/EQD/NRR—2012/490. National Park Service, Fort Collins, Colorado.

Kulesza, C., Y. Le, and S.J. Hollenhorst. 2012b. Congaree National Park Visitor Study, Summer 2011. Natural Resource Report NPS/NRSS/EQD/NRR—2012/565. National Park Service, Fort Collins, Colorado.

MIG, Inc. 2008. IMPLAN Professional Version 3.0. Minnesota IMPLAN Group: Stillwater, MN.

National Park Service Public Use Statistics Office. 2011. Visitation Database. http://www2.nature.nps.gov/stats/. Data retrieved on September 26, 2012.

Samuelson, M., Y. Le, and S.J. Hollenhorst. 2012a. Congaree National Park Visitor Study, Fall 2011. Natural Resource Report NPS/NRSS/EQD/NRR—2012/607. National Park Service, Fort Collins, Colorado.

Samuelson, M., Y. Le, and S.J. Hollenhorst. 2012b. Congaree National Park Visitor Study, Winter 2012. Natural Resource Report NPS/NRSS/EQD/NRR—2012/608. National Park Service, Fort Collins, Colorado.

Stynes, D. J. 2011. Economic Benefits to Local Communities from National Park Visitation and Payroll, 2010. NPS/NRSS/EQD/NRR—2011/481. National Park Service, Fort Collins, Colorado.

Stynes, D. J., D.B. Propst, W. Chang, and Y. Sun. 2007. NPS Money Generation Model – Version 2 (MGM2). http://mgm2impact.com/MGM2Y2011.xls (with price indices updated to 2011).

USCB (U.S. Census Bureau). 2011. American FactFinder. http://factfinder2.census.gov/faces/nav/jsf/pages/index.xhtml. Data retrieved on September 26, 2012.

Appendix A: Glossary

Term	Definition
Direct effects	Changes in sales, income and jobs in those business or agencies that directly receive visitor spending.
Economic multiplier	Captures the size of secondary effects and are usually expressed as a ratio of total effects to direct effects.
Economic ratio	Converts various economic measures from one to another. For example, direct sales can be used to estimate direct effects on jobs, personal income, and value added by applying economic ratios. That is: • Direct jobs = direct sales * jobs to sales ratio • Direct personal income = direct sales * personal income to sales ratio • Direct value added = direct sales * value added to sales ratio.
Indirect effects	Changes in sales, income and jobs in industries that supply goods and services to the businesses that sell directly to visitors, i.e., businesses in the supply chain. For example, linen suppliers benefit from visitor spending at motels.
Induced effects	Changes in economic activity in the region resulting from household spending of income earned through a direct or indirect effect of visitor spending. For example, motel and linen supply employees live in the region and spend their incomes on housing, groceries, education, clothing and other goods and services. IMPLAN's Social Accounting Matrix (SAM) multipliers also include induced effects resulting from local/state/federal government spending.
Jobs	The number of jobs in the region supported by visitor spending. Job estimates are not full time equivalents, but include both fulltime and part-time positions.
Labor income	Wage and salary income, sole proprietor (business owner) income and employee payroll benefits.
Regional purchase coefficient (RPC)	The proportion of demand within a region supplied by producers within that region.
Retail margin	The markup to the price of a product when a product is sold through a retail trade activity. Retail margin is calculated as sales receipts minus the cost of goods sold.
Sales	Direct sales (retail goods and services) of firms within the region to park visitors.

Term	Definition
Secondary effects	Changes in the economic activity in the region that result from the re-circulation of money spent by visitors. Secondary effects include indirect and induced effects.
Total effects	Sum of direct, indirect and induced effects. • Direct effects accrue largely to tourism-related businesses in the area. • Indirect effects accrue to a broader set of businesses that serve these tourism firms. • Induced effects are distributed widely across a variety of local businesses.
Value added	Labor income plus property income (rents, dividends, royalties, interest) and indirect business taxes. As the name implies, it is the net value added to the region's economy. For example, the value added by a motel includes wages and salaries paid to employees, their payroll benefits, profits of the motel, and sales, property, and other indirect business taxes. The motel's non-labor operating costs such as purchases of supplies and services from other firms are not included as value added by the motel.
Visitor group	A group of people traveling together to visit the park. Visitor group is the basic sampling unit for VSP surveys; each visitor group receives only one questionnaire.
Wholesale margin	The markup to the price of a product when a product is sold through wholesale trade. Wholesale margin is calculated as wholesale sales minus the cost of the goods sold.

Appendix B: Expenditure Sector Assignments

Table B1 shows expenditure categories visitors were asked to estimate in the Congaree NP VSP questionnaires. Some expenditure categories were combined and renamed for MGM2 analysis.

Table B1. Expenditure categories in Congaree NP questionnaires and MGM2 sector assignment

Questionnaire expenditure categories	Inside park	Outside park	MGM2 sector
Lodges, hotels, motels, cabins, B&B, etc.		X	Motels
Camping fees and charges		X	Camping fees
Canoe/kayak rental charges		X	Admissions & fees
Guide fees and charges		X	Admissions & fees
Restaurants and bars		X	Restaurants & bars
Groceries and takeout food		X	Groceries & takeout food
Gas and oil (auto, RV, boat, etc.)		X	Gas & oil
Other transportation expenses (rental cars, taxis, auto repairs, but NOT airfare)		X	Local transportation
Admission, recreation, entertainment fees		X	Admissions & fees
All other purchases (souvenirs, film, books, sporting goods, clothing, etc.)	X	X	Souvenirs & other expenses
Donations	X	X	Souvenirs & other expenses

X = category included in questionnaire.

MGM2 sectors names correspond to similar sector names and numbers in IMPLAN (Table B2). IMPLAN sectors also correspond to 2007 North American Industry Classification System (NAICS) sectors.

Table B2. MGM2 sector correspondence to IMPLAN and 2007 NAICS sectors

MGM2 sector	IMPLAN No.	IMPLAN Name	2007 NAICS
Motels	411	Hotels and motels, including casino hotels	72111-2
Camping fees	412	Other accommodations	72119, 7212-3
Restaurants & bars	413	Food services and drinking places	722
Groceries & takeout food	324	Retail - Food and beverage	445
Gas & oil	326	Retail - Gasoline stations	447
Local transportation	336	Transit and ground passenger transportation	485
Admissions & fees	410	Other amusement and recreation industries	71391-3, 71399
Souvenirs & other expenses	329	Retail - General merchandise	452
Local production of goods	317	All other miscellaneous manufacturing	339993, 339995, 339999
Wholesale trade	319	Wholesale trade	42

Source: IMPLAN (MIG, Inc. 2008).

Appendix C: Economic Ratios and Multipliers

Table C1. Economic ratios and multipliers for selected tourism-related sectors, Congaree NP region, 2011

Sector	Direct effects				Total effects multipliers				
	Jobs /$MM sales	Income /sales	Value added/ sales	Sales I	Sales SAM	Job II/ MM sales	Income II/ sales	Value added II/sales
Motels	13.57	0.30	0.53	1.34	1.66	19.16	0.50	0.88
Camping fees	11.98	0.32	0.52	1.38	1.66	17.93	0.53	0.88
Restaurants & bars	19.17	0.34	0.49	1.33	1.64	24.22	0.53	0.83
Groceries & takeout food	18.80	0.51	0.83	1.29	1.66	24.36	0.71	1.20
Gas & oil	18.03	0.50	0.83	1.25	1.53	22.46	0.66	1.13
Local transportation	31.08	0.43	0.54	1.23	1.56	35.95	0.61	0.84
Admission & fees	18.93	0.37	0.57	1.51	1.76	25.28	0.60	0.98
Souvenirs & other expenses	20.91	0.51	0.83	1.29	1.67	26.54	0.72	1.21
Local production of goods	6.42	0.23	0.36	1.25	1.50	10.23	0.38	0.63
Wholesale trade	5.74	0.38	0.65	1.27	1.62	11.09	0.58	1.00

Source: IMPLAN (MIG, Inc. 2008) updated to 2011.

Explanation of table

Direct effects are economic ratios to convert sales in each sector to jobs, income and value added.

> Jobs/$MM sales is jobs per million dollars in sales.
> Income/sales is the percentage of sales going to wages, salaries, and employee benefits.
> Value added/sales is the percentage of sales that is value added (Value added covers all income, rents and profits and indirect business taxes).

Total effects are multipliers that capture the total effect relative to direct sales.

> Sales I captures only direct and indirect sales.
> Sales SAM is the SAM sales multiplier = (direct + indirect + induced sales) /direct sales.
> Job II/ MM sales = total jobs (direct + indirect + induced) per $ million in direct sales.
> Income II /sales = total income (direct + indirect + induced) per $ of direct sales.
> Value added II/sales = total value added (direct + indirect + induced) per $ of direct sales.

Using the motels sector row to illustrate

Direct Effects: Every million dollars in motel sales creates 13.6 jobs in motels. Fifty-three percent of motel sales are value added, including 30% that goes to wages and salaries of motel employees. That means 47% of motel sales goes to purchase inputs by motels (e.g., linens, cleaning supplies). The wage and salary income creates the induced effects and the 47% spent on purchases by the motel starts the rounds of indirect effects.

Multiplier effects: There is an additional 34 cents of indirect sales in the region for every dollar of direct motel sales (type I sales multiplier = 1.34). Total secondary sales are 66 cents per dollar of direct sales, which means 34 cents in indirect effects and 32 cents in induced effects. An additional 5.6 jobs are created from secondary effects of each million dollars in motel sales (19.2 total jobs – 13.6 direct jobs per million dollars). These jobs are distributed across other sectors of the local economy. Similarly, the secondary effects on income for each dollar of motel sales are 20% (50%-30%), and the secondary effects on value added for each dollar of motel sales are 35% (88%-53%). Including secondary effects, every million dollars of motel sales in the region yields $1.66 million in sales, which supports 19.2 jobs. Those jobs pay $580,000 in labor income, which is part of the overall value added of $1,000,000.

Appendix D: Comparison of Spring, Summer, Fall, and Winter Visitors

Visitor segment percentages and trip characteristics are similar between the seasonal samples (Table D1). However, summer visitor groups tended to be slightly larger and stay slightly longer than visitor groups in other seasons.

Table D1. Visitor segment mix and conversion factors, by season

Characteristic	Local	Day trip	Camp-in	Motel-out	Camp-out	Other OVN	All visitors
Spring							
Visitor segment share (park entries)	29%	29%	6%	24%	2%	10%	100%
Average visitor group size	2.8	2.5	2.1	2.1	1.8	2.3	2.4
Length of stay (days or nights)	1.0	1.0	1.0	1.8	2.4	2.0	1.8
Re-entry rate (park entries per trip)	1.0	1.0	1.1	1.0	1.0	1.0	1.0
Percent primary purpose trips	100%	77%	83%	62%	60%	50%	68%
Summer							
Visitor segment share (park entries)	24%	38%	2%	22%	2%	12%	100%
Average visitor group size	2.9	2.9	4.3	2.4	2.0	2.3	2.7
Length of stay (days or nights)	1.0	1.0	1.0	1.9	2.8	2.6	2.1
Re-entry rate (park entries per trip)	1.0	1.0	1.1	1.0	1.1	1.1	1.0
Percent primary purpose trips	100%	56%	100%	47%	75%	30%	50%
Fall							
Visitor segment share (park entries)	35%	29%	5%	19%	4%	8%	100%
Average visitor group size	2.7	2.6	2.8	2.6	2.2	2.7	2.6
Length of stay (days or nights)	1.0	1.0	1.2	1.6	1.4	2.2	1.8
Re-entry rate (park entries per trip)	1.0	1.0	1.4	1.0	1.1	1.4	1.1
Percent primary purpose trips	100%	72%	100%	70%	60%	56%	70%
Winter							
Visitor segment share (park entries)	30%	35%	6%	20%	1%	8%	100%
Average visitor group size	2.2	2.5	2.3	2.2	4.0	2.4	2.3
Length of stay (days or nights)	1.0	1.0	1.0	1.7	1.2	2.5	1.9
Re-entry rate (park entries per trip)	1.0	1.0	1.1	1.0	1.2	1.2	1.0
Percent primary purpose trips	100%	70%	86%	69%	67%	45%	67%

Differences in spending patterns between seasons reflect the larger visitor group sizes and longer stays of summer visitors (Tables D2, D3, D4, and D5).

Table D2. Average visitor spending by segment, dollars per visitor group per trip, spring 2011

| | Segment | | | | | | |
Expenditures	Local	Day trip	Camp-in*	Motel-out	Camp-out*	Other OVN	All visitors**
Inside park							
Souvenirs & other expenses	3.29	3.72	2.30	5.32	0.80	2.32	3.74
Total inside park	**3.29**	**3.72**	**2.30**	**5.32**	**0.80**	**2.32**	**3.74**
Outside park							
Motels	0.00	0.00	0.00	152.39	0.00	0.00	41.74
Camping fees	0.00	0.00	0.00	0.00	39.60	0.00	1.07
Restaurants & bars	3.64	9.19	9.20	78.81	14.00	22.28	28.31
Groceries & takeout food	2.07	4.18	5.40	8.48	30.00	14.12	6.61
Gas & oil	12.36	20.19	25.52	50.95	72.00	36.39	29.99
Local Transportation	0.22	0.40	0.00	11.31	0.00	0.00	3.27
Admission & fees	3.29	1.88	0.00	5.00	0.00	1.12	2.85
Souvenirs & other expenses	0.27	2.61	3.45	13.89	6.00	9.36	5.94
Total outside park	**21.85**	**38.46**	**43.56**	**320.83**	**161.60**	**83.28**	**119.78**
Total inside & outside park	**25.14**	**42.18**	**45.86**	**326.15**	**162.40**	**85.60**	**123.52**

*Only 10 visitor groups reported camping inside the park and 9 visitor groups reported camping outside the park. Results should be interpreted with caution due to small sample sizes.

**Weighted by percent visitor group trips.

Table D3. Average visitor spending by segment, dollars per visitor group per trip, summer 2011

| | Segment | | | | | | |
Expenditures	Local	Day trip	Camp-in*	Motel-out	Camp-out*	Other OVN	All visitors**
Inside park							
Souvenirs & other expenses	1.87	4.70	21.78	8.39	18.57	13.29	6.62
Total inside park	**1.87**	**4.70**	**21.78**	**8.39**	**18.57**	**13.29**	**6.62**
Outside park							
Motels	0.00	0.00	0.00	166.35	0.00	0.00	40.69
Camping fees	0.00	0.00	0.00	0.31	81.43	0.00	2.03
Restaurants & bars	7.39	16.12	22.22	69.79	64.29	16.59	28.55
Groceries & takeout food	6.09	5.33	11.11	16.76	71.43	9.51	10.50
Gas & oil	9.73	24.38	13.33	73.80	154.29	22.63	35.89
Local Transportation	0.00	0.00	0.00	42.59	28.57	0.77	11.20
Admission & fees	2.36	6.43	0.00	10.88	85.71	3.35	8.01
Souvenirs & other expenses	1.13	3.76	19.56	19.50	28.57	2.88	7.67
Total outside park	**26.71**	**56.01**	**66.22**	**399.99**	**514.29**	**55.73**	**144.54**
Total inside & outside park	**28.58**	**60.71**	**88.00**	**408.39**	**532.86**	**69.03**	**151.16**

*Only 2 visitor groups reported camping inside the park and 6 visitor groups reported camping outside the park. Results should be interpreted with caution due to small sample sizes.

**Weighted by percent visitor group trips.

Table D4. Average visitor spending by segment, dollars per visitor group per trip, fall 2011

Expenditures	Local	Day trip	Camp-in*	Motel-out	Camp-out*	Other OVN	All visitors**
Inside park							
Souvenirs & other expenses	3.27	5.65	6.86	6.65	5.56	4.88	4.98
Total inside park	**3.27**	**5.65**	**6.86**	**6.65**	**5.56**	**4.88**	**4.98**
Outside park							
Motels	0.00	0.00	0.00	152.13	0.00	0.00	29.96
Camping fees	0.00	0.00	0.00	0.00	46.09	0.00	2.13
Restaurants & bars	5.08	10.58	7.25	72.34	20.29	10.33	21.08
Groceries & takeout food	3.19	2.06	16.02	12.37	27.94	14.76	6.89
Gas & oil	7.23	22.06	27.50	49.57	75.88	36.18	25.60
Local Transportation	0.00	0.28	0.00	17.79	13.24	0.51	4.23
Admission & fees	0.00	0.28	0.00	8.74	2.47	5.30	2.22
Souvenirs & other expenses	2.56	2.38	42.02	14.82	9.79	1.53	6.54
Total outside park	**18.06**	**37.63**	**92.79**	**327.75**	**195.71**	**68.61**	**98.66**
Total inside & outside park	**21.33**	**43.28**	**99.65**	**334.40**	**201.26**	**73.49**	**103.64**

*Only 12 visitor groups reported camping inside the park and 13 visitor groups reported camping outside the park. Results should be interpreted with caution due to small sample sizes.

**Weighted by percent visitor group trips.

Table D5. Average visitor spending by segment, dollars per visitor group per trip, winter 2012

Expenditures	Local	Day trip	Camp-in*	Motel-out	Camp-out*	Other OVN	All visitors**
Inside park							
Souvenirs & other expenses	1.86	3.54	2.74	6.28	12.40	4.00	3.62
Total inside park	**1.86**	**3.54**	**2.74**	**6.28**	**12.40**	**4.00**	**3.62**
Outside park							
Motels	0.00	0.00	0.00	159.30	0.00	0.00	34.69
Camping fees	0.00	0.00	0.00	0.00	34.40	0.00	0.17
Restaurants & bars	5.02	10.52	15.38	66.06	26.00	11.94	21.28
Groceries & takeout food	4.14	3.18	17.37	11.54	5.00	24.62	7.58
Gas & oil	7.19	23.37	24.09	45.95	130.00	25.06	23.70
Local Transportation	0.00	6.86	0.00	4.78	0.00	3.74	3.54
Admission & fees	0.00	0.42	1.08	4.05	2.00	0.90	1.15
Souvenirs & other expenses	1.28	0.89	2.69	9.98	16.60	20.18	4.47
Total outside park	**17.63**	**45.24**	**60.59**	**301.66**	**214.00**	**86.44**	**96.58**
Total inside & outside park	**19.48**	**48.77**	**63.33**	**307.94**	**226.40**	**90.44**	**100.19**

*Only 15 visitor groups reported camping inside the park and 4 visitor groups reported camping outside the park. Results should be interpreted with caution due to small sample sizes.

**Weighted by percent visitor group trips.

Spending averages for visitor groups throughout the year were computed by weighting seasonal spending averages by the percentage of visits occurring during each season.

The Department of the Interior protects and manages the nation's natural resources and cultural heritage; provides scientific and other information about those resources; and honors its special responsibilities to American Indians, Alaska Natives, and affiliated Island Communities.

NPS 178/119428, January 2013